# COOK-LIKE-A-STUD

*38 lip smackin' meals men can prepare in the garage ... using their own tools!

## Ross Shafer

**Woodland Hills, California • Jester Books**

# Dedicated

to my beautiful
and talented wife

## Paula

who has always
smiled and hugged
me in the face
of a thousand
off center adventures
like this one

# Foreword

This recent effort at cooking by my friend Ross Shafer is disgusting! I have spent ten years trying to get macho men out of the garage and into the kitchen. Now, Shafer wants these men to move from the kitchen back to the garage.

However, the book is incredibly funny and it may just help my efforts at freeing men to cook. After all, Ross looks like a stud and yet he is really not bad in the kitchen ... cooking, I mean.

But Ross, slicing a meatloaf with a chain saw?

Come on!

**Jeff Smith**
The Frugal Gourmet

# Introduction

Women say men should cook more often. There are two reasons we don't. First, we don't look very "studly" when we do it. God forbid our male friends should catch us in an apron. We'd be laughed right off the *Field & Stream* mailing list. Secondly, we truly cannot decipher the two hundred different cooking utensils and measuring devices in the kitchen, most of which are hidden in sixteen secret drawers throughout the kitchen and dining room. And, since most women won't let us hang their kitchen tools out in the open on pegboard, I felt the need to spearhead the now famous men's cooking revolution. The revolution is dedicated to a simple credo: "Let us cook in the garage using the tools we know and love." (Of course, if you can sneak in and use the oven, go for it.) The result is a cookbook full of recipes any man can follow with absolutely no risk to his masculinity.

It almost brings a tear to my eye ... almost.

**R.S.**

# Acknowledgements

My sincere gratitude to Douglas Dunn, Jan Frazier, Michelle Marx, John and Merrily Keister, Ken Sax, Jeff Smith, Chuck, Lois, Scott, Clell, Adam and Ryan Shafer, Sam, Beverly and Mark Meln, all my "Match Game" buddies, David Brady, Irvin Arthur, John Powell, Steve Katleman, Jim Sharp, Howard and Patti Bolter and the whole gang at K.N.I.

Some of you had nothing to do with this book but I thought it was an opportune time to thank you for making my life such a gas!

# "Stud" Cooking Preparation

# Don't Wear This...

Anyone Who Says 'One Size Fits All' Hasn't Met Me

# ...Wear **This**

Stud men don't wear aprons with silly sayings on them. Instead, wear a tank top you got on vacation or one you saved from college. Your biceps will look much more awesome when you're pounding, dicing, cutting, crushing, grating and grinding the food.

Accessorize the tank top with an authentic journeyman carpenter's tool belt and you've got the full stud man cooking ensemble that drives women wild.

# Stud Man Cooking Tools

### Roofing Hammer
Tenderizing meat

### Hatchet
Chops vegetables, fruit and meat

### Utility Knife
Cuts excess fat and slices thin

### Bench Vise
Perfect for holding vegetables and cheese when grating

### Body & Fender File
World's Best cheese and rind grater

### Cement Trowel
A sturdier spatula

### Paint Stirrer Stick
Blends everything

### Hack Saw
Bones don't stand a chance

### Hand Saw
Easy for cutting thick meats

### Paint Roller & Brush
Fast, full coverage basting

### Propane Torch
The backbone of garage cooking when an oven or stove isn't available

### Bench Grinder
Peels skin off fruit and vegetables

### Power Drill
Use with a 1" spade bit to whip potatoes, gravies and sauces

# Stud Man Cookery Essentials

 **Coffee Cans**
Use assorted sizes for
mixing ingredients

 **Paint Tray**
Use as a frying pan and
baking dish

 **Steel Oil Drain Pan**
Good for baking
most anything

 **Short Block Oil Pan**
Best for casseroles and
as a roaster when high
heat is required

# Measurements

We don't have time to fuss with teaspoons and one third cups.
Here are some measurements we understand.

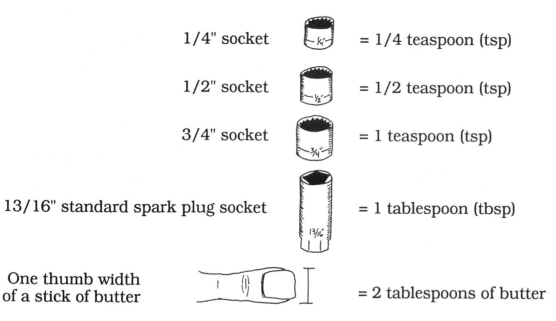

1/4" socket = 1/4 teaspoon (tsp)

1/2" socket = 1/2 teaspoon (tsp)

3/4" socket = 1 teaspoon (tsp)

13/16" standard spark plug socket = 1 tablespoon (tbsp)

One thumb width
of a stick of butter = 2 tablespoons of butter

# **Measurements** (Continued)

1 shot glass full to the rim  = 1/4 cup

2 shot glasses  = 1/2 cup

1/2 beer can  = 1 cup

Almost full tennis ball can  = 3 cups

Small handful  = 1/3 cup Dry Ingredients

Heaping handful  = 1/3 cup Dry Ingredients

# APPETIZERS

# Emergency Hors D'Oeuvres

You never know when rude friends will drop over without notice. So, be prepared with this appetizer you can throw together in fifteen seconds. It tastes so good your guests will never suspect you despise them.

**Tools required**:   Swiss Army knife can opener.

| Ingredients | "Stud" measurement | Kitchen Equivalent |
| --- | --- | --- |
| Cream Cheese | 1   8-oz. pkg. | 1 8-oz. pkg. |
| Canned Crab | 1 small can | 1 small can |
| Seafood cocktail sauce | 1 small bottle | 1 small bottle |
| Trisket Crackers | 1 box | 1 box |

Put the block of cream cheese on a serving plate. Toss the whole can of crab on top of the cheese. Pour the bottle of cocktail sauce over the crab and cheese. Serve with sturdy crackers.

10

# Macho Nachos

Everybody loves nachos. I never feel guilty about their nutritional value because all the food groups are represented! Chase with cold beer.

**Tools required**:   vise, body file, paint tray, torch

| Ingredients | "Stud" measurement | Kitchen Equivalent |
|---|---|---|
| Tortilla Chips | 2 lb. pkg. | 2 lb. pkg |
| Monterey Jack Cheese (grated) | 1/2 beer can | 1 cup |
| Cheddar Cheese (grated) | 1/2 beer can | 1 cup |
| Mozzarella Cheese (grated) | 1/2 beer can | 1 cup |
| Ground beef | 1 lb. | 1 lb. |
| Guacamole | 2 shot glasses | 1/2 cup |
| Salsa | 2 shot glasses | 1/2 cup |
| Sour Cream | 1 shot glass | 1/4 cup |

Brown the ground beef in your paint tray. Drain off grease. Grate the cheeses with your body file. Spread the tortilla chips one layer thick in another paint tray. Cover the chips with mozzarella. Layer the ground beef on top of the mozzarella. Sprinkle cheddar and Jack cheese on top of the ground beef. Torch or bake at about 400° for 15 minutes. Don't let the cheese burn. Serve with guacamole, salsa and sour cream on the side.

12

# Dance With the Deviled Eggs

You can go to any wedding reception, family reunion or holiday party and these are always the first to go. Which tells me that people are willing to endanger their cholesterol level for a taste of this sinful treat. I love people who live on the edge.

**Tools required**:   Coffee can, utility knife, hammer, putty knife

| Ingredients | "Stud" measurement | Kitchen Equivalent |
|---|---|---|
| Eggs (hard boiled) | 12 | 12 |
| Mayonnaise | 2 shot glasses | $1/2$ cup |
| Mustard | half shot glass | $1/8$ cup |
| Curry powder | Spark plug socket | 1 tbsp |
| Salt & pepper | A little | To taste |

Boil the eggs in a coffee can. Hammer the shell off. Cut the eggs lengthwise. Take the yolks out and put in another can. Add mayonnaise, mustard, curry powder, salt and pepper. Mash it all together until smooth. Use your putty knife to fill the egg hole. Sprinkle a little paprika on top if you're artistic.

14

# Yuppie Brie and Almonds

This is one of my favorites because it makes my hot shot lawyer and stock broker buddies think I'm hip. What they don't know is that I prepare it right next to my weed whacker.

**Tools required**:  3" hole saw, paint tray or coffee can, utility knife.

| Ingredients | "Stud" measurement | Kitchen Equivalent |
|---|---|---|
| Brie Cheese | 6 - 8 oz. block | 6 - 8 oz. block |
| Butter (stick) | 1 thumb width | 2 tbsp |
| Toasted almonds (pulverized) | 2 shot glasses | $1/2$ cup |
| Crackers | Enough | $1/2$ box |

Use your hole saw to cut a 3" circle of brie out of the block. Let stand at room temperature for one hour. Melt the butter in a coffee can with your torch and pour over the cheese. Slice the almonds with your knife and sprinkle over the top.Serve with crackers and plenty of talk about downside risk and litigation.

# Chisled Chinese Pork

This appetizer is good even without Chinese food. It also makes killer sandwiches later. For you heart patients, no pun intended.

**Tools required**:   3" wood chisel, hammer, oil pan, paint brush.

| Ingredients | "Stud" measurement | Kitchen Equivalent |
|---|---|---|
| Pork loin roast | 2 - 3 lbs. | 2 - 3 lbs. |
| Meat marinade | 1 pkg. | 1 pkg. |
| Toasted sesame seeds | 2 shot glasses | 1/2 cup |
| Hot mustard | 1 shot glass | 1/4 cup |

Soak (marinate) the roast according to the instructions on the package. Then torch or cook the roast at 325° for 1 1/2 hours. Paint the roast with the marinade every 30 minutes while cooking. Let cool and chisel off bite size hunks. Serve with sesame seeds, hot mustard and plenty of water in case you get too cocky with the mustard.

# SALADS

# Samurai Chef's Salad

By the time you finish slicing, dicing and hacking your way through this light meal, you'll be a world class Ninja salad master.

**Tools required**:    machete or samurai sword

| Ingredients | "Stud" measurement | Kitchen Equivalent |
|---|:---:|:---:|
| Iceberg lettuce | 1 head | 1 head |
| Ham (cooked) | 1 beer can | 1/2 lb. |
| Turkey (cooked) | 1 beer can | 1/2 lb. |
| Celery | 2 shot glasses | 1/2 cup |
| Onions | 2 shot glasses | 1/2 cup |
| Bacon bits | 1 shot glass | 1/4 cup |
| Tomatoes | 2 | 2 |
| Swiss cheese | 1 beer can | 1/2 lb. |

Use your machete to chop and slice all ingredients in no particular order. Heave everything into a large serving bowl. There is no way you can screw this up. Serve with your favorite dressings.

20

# Sky High Society Waldorf Fruit Salad

From New York City's world famous Waldorf Astoria hotel to the comfort of your garage. Tastes great and low in calories. This baby impresses women!

**Tools required**:   hatchet or axe, paint stirrer

| Ingredients | "Stud" measurement | Kitchen Equivalent |
|---|---|---|
| Apple chunks | 1 full beer can | 2 cups |
| Celery | $^1/_2$ beer can | 1 cup |
| Walnuts (chopped) | 2 shot glasses | $^1/_2$ cup |
| Mayonnaise | 2 shot glasses | $^1/_2$ cup |
| Raisins | 2 shot glasses | $^1/_2$ cup |

Raise your axe and hack up the apples, celery and walnuts. Toss them all in a large bowl with the mayonnaise and raisins. Stir it all until blended and serve on a small plate. Then tell your wife, girlfriend or date her mouth is gaped open.

# BREADS

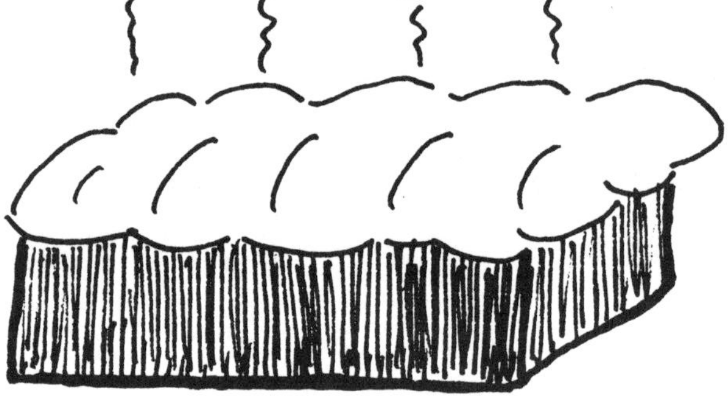

# Homemade Holesaw Biscuits

I can't flip an egg without shattering the yolk. And, I always overfry bacon into ashes. But, I am awesome at biscuits. I'm only sorry there is no Biscuit Olympics.

**Tools required**:   2" hole saw, oil pan, coffee can

| Ingredients | "Stud" measurement | Kitchen Equivalent |
|---|---|---|
| Flour | 1 full beer can | 2 cups. |
| Baking powder | 3 $3/4$" sockets | 3 tsps |
| Salt | $3/4$" socket | 1 tsp. |
| Butter | 1 thumb width of butter stick | 2 tbsps. |
| Milk | 3 shot glasses | $3/4$ cup |

Combine all ingredients in a large coffee can until soft and dough-like. Flatten dough on your workbench until dough is one inch thick. Use your hole saw to cut circles in dough. Put circles in a paint tray and torch or bake at 300° for 8-12 minutes until biscuits are golden brown. Puff out your chest and serve immediately. No need to be modest.

24

# Friday the 13th Pumpkin Bread

Nobody will believe you made this yourself. It's perfect for Halloween office gifts. Especially if you deliver it wearing a hockey mask.

**Tools required**:  Swiss Army knife can opener or a sharp utility knife. Small valve cover.

| Ingredients | "Stud" measurement | Kitchen Equivalent |
| --- | --- | --- |
| Wesson oil | $1/2$ beer can | 1 cup |
| Sugar | 1 heaping full tennis ball can | 4 cups |
| Libby's canned pumpkin | 1 large can | 1 lb. 13 oz. |
| Flour | $2^1/2$ beer cans | 5 cups |
| Cinnamon | 2 $3/4$" sockets | 2 tsp. |
| Cloves | $3/4$" socket | 1 tsp. |
| Salt | $3/4$" socket | 1 tsp. |
| Baking Soda | 4 $3/4$" sockets | 4 tsp. |
| Walnuts | 1 beer can | 2 cups |

In one oil pan, mix the oil, sugar and pumpkin. In another oil pan combine flour, cinnamon, cloves,salt and baking soda. Add this to the first oil pan mixture. Last, stir in the walnuts. Pour into a valve cover or loaf pan. Torch or bake at 350° for one hour.

# SIDE DISHES

# Bench Vise Vegetable Bake

Mom said eat your greens. This spinach and broccoli dish will fool you into thinking you actually like them.

**Tools required**:   Bench vise, body file, oil pan

| Ingredients | "Stud" measurement | Kitchen Equivalent |
|---|---|---|
| Spinach | 1 bunch | 1 bunch |
| Broccoli | 1 bunch | 1 bunch |
| Cheddar cheese | 1/2 beer can | 1 cup |
| Sour cream | 1 small dairy case size | 1 pint |
| Lipton Onion Soup | 1 pkg. | 1 pkg. |

Boil spinach and broccoli in your oil pan for 20 minutes. Drain off water. Put spinach and broccoli in your bench vise and squeeze out excess water. Combine the sour cream, add onion soup mix with the veggies in a short block oil pan or baking dish. Grate the cheese with your body file and sprinkle cheese over the top. Torch or bake at 350° for 45 minutes. This is easily three times as good as it sounds.

28

# Mallet Mashed Potatoes

We forget we don't have to wait for a holiday. Mashed potatoes are good anytime. I made some just to help me cope with an episode of Oprah.

**Tools required**:   wood or rubber mallet, oil pan, bench grinder, axe

| Ingredients | "Stud" measurement | Kitchen Equivalent |
|---|---|---|
| Russet potatoes | 20 | 20 |
| Butter | 1 thumb width of butter stick | 2 tbsps. |
| Salt | 3/4" socket | 1 tsp. |
| Milk | 1 shot glass | 1/4 cup |

Grind the skins off your potatoes with your bench grinder. Hack each spud twice with your axe and submerge in your oil pan of boiling water for 30 minutes. Drain off the water. Add butter, milk and salt. Mash everything with your mallet until you like the consistency. If you are fussy about lumps, attach a 1" blade bit to your power drill and whip the spuds 'til smooth. Eat.

# Karate Chopped Broccoli

You know how many times you ask, "Can I help with dinner?" You may not really mean it but here's a side dish that will score points for our side. It can easily be made during commercial breaks.

**Tools required**:   Axe, body file & vise, oil pan.

| Ingredients | "Stud" measurement | Kitchen Equivalent |
|---|---|---|
| Frozen Broccoli (thawed) | 3 freezer pkgs. | 3 freezer pkgs. |
| Cream of chicken soup | 2 regular size cans | 2 11 oz.cans |
| Eggs (beaten) | 4 | 4 |
| Sharp cheddar cheese | $1/2$ beer can and 2 shot glasses | $1^1/2$ cups |

As the broccoli is thawing I like to separate it with my deadly fists of fury. Then chop it up with your axe and mix all ingredients together in your oil pan. Torch or bake at 350° for one hour. Soak your bruised hands in ice for 20 minutes.

32

# Butter de la Peanut Green Beans

When a friend of mine served peanut butter sauce on green beans I thought it was a practical joke. I played along. I loved them! Then, I tried his gingerbread corn casserole. That was the practical joke.

**Tools required**:   Oil pan, utility knife, coffee can

| Ingredients | "Stud" measurement | Kitchen Equivalent |
|---|---|---|
| Green beans | 5 heaping handfuls | 4 cups |
| Peanut Butter (chunky style) | 4 standard spark plug sockets | 4 tbsps. |
| Dry Sherry | 4 standard spark plug sockets | 4 tbsps. |
| Oyster sauce | 4 $^3/_4$" sockets | 4 tsps. |
| Ginger root (minced) | 1 $^3/_4$" socket | 1 tsp. |

Cook beans in boiling water (use your oil pan) for 20 minutes. In a medium coffee can combine peanut butter, sherry, oyster sauce, and ginger root. Torch to a boil. Reduce flame and simmer peanut butter sauce until creamy. Pour over hot beans and serve. Can you believe I fell for a gingerbread corn casserole? Neither could the doctor who pumped my stomach.

# Ragin' Cajun Chicken

Hot, spicy and simple. And, you can get it ready and let it cook for an entire football game. If the game goes into overtime, the chicken shouldn't.

**Tools required**:  paint tray, hatchet

| Ingredients | "Stud" measurement | Kitchen Equivalent |
|---|---|---|
| Chicken parts | 3 lbs. | 3 lbs. |
| Polish sausage | 12" (chopped) | 1 ring |
| Butter | 1 thumb width of butter stick | 2 tbsps. |
| Green pepper | 1 chopped | 1 |
| Red pepper | 1 chopped | 1 |
| White onion | 1 chopped | 1 |
| Canned tomatoes | 1 can | 1 can |
| Cayenne pepper | 3/4" socket | 1 tsp. |
| Water | 2 shot glasses | 1/2 cup |

Melt butter in the paint tray or oil pan and cook chopped peppers and onion until limp. Add chicken parts, sausage, cayenne, tomatoes and water. Cover it with something and walk away for 1½ hours. Cooking temp should be 350°. Ah, tasty over rice or potato chips.

# Jig Sawed Chicken Nuggets

This is for finger food lovers. Translation — bachelors who hate to do dishes.

**Tools required**:   Jig saw, paint tray, trowel, coffee can

| Ingredients | "Stud" measurement | Kitchen Equivalent |
|---|---|---|
| Boneless & skinless chicken breasts | 6 | 6 |
| Egg | 1 | 1 |
| Onion soup mix | 1 | 1 |
| Dried bread crumbs | 2 shot glasses | $^1/_2$ cup |

Use your jig saw to cut the breasts into 1" squares. You can cut them into animal or building shapes if you're really clever. Combine the beaten egg, the soup mix, and half the bread crumbs in a coffee can. Then wallow each nugget in the mixture. Place nuggets in your paint tray and top with remaining crumbs. Torch or bake for 10 minutes at 400°. Turn the nuggets over with your trowel and cook the other side. That's it. Dip in ketchup or BBQ sauce until you're full.

38

# Hammered Chicken Breasts

This is the recipe that started the "Stud" cooking craze. We ate this dish at John and Merrily Keister's house and it was delicious. Merrily is a multi-media artist and loves to pound things. John loves Merrily and humors her behavior.

**Tools required**:   Drywall or roofing hammer, body file and vise, coffee can, paint tray

| Ingredients | "Stud" measurement | Kitchen Equivalent |
| --- | --- | --- |
| Boneless, skinless chicken breasts | 2 | 2 |
| Parmesan cheese | 2 shot glasses | $1/2$ cup (grated) |
| Parsley | 2 shot glasses | $1/2$ cup (chopped) |
| Black pepper | A little | $1/4$ tsp. |
| Butter | 2 thumb width of butter stick | 4 tbsps. |
| Dry Sherry | 1 shot glass | $1/4$ cup |

Place breasts on a large piece of tarp. Chop and file the cheese and parsley. In a small coffee can, combine the cheese, pepper and parsley. Put half this mixture on the breasts and cover with another piece of tarp. Hammer the breasts until they flatten to $1/4"$ thickness. Turn over and repeat with remaining cheese mixture. Melt butter in a paint tray or skillet, add breasts and torch at medium heat for 3-4 minutes on each side. During the last 2 minutes add sherry until slightly thickened. Hey, you just made a sauce to pour over chicken. Serve and thank Merrily Keister!

# Hefty Bag Fried Chicken

I got a good buy on 100 garbage bags once. I didn't think I'd ever get rid of all of them. Then, I saw how fried chicken was made. Now, I'm shopping for a good deal on another hundred bags.

**Tools required**:   Axe, Hefty bag, paint tray, oil pan

| Ingredients | "Stud" measurement | Kitchen Equivalent |
|---|---|---|
| Whole chickens | 2 | 2 |
| Butter | 1 thumb width of butter stick | 2 tbsps. |
| Flour | 2 small handfuls | $^2/_3$ cup |
| Seasoning salt | 2 $^3/_4$" sockets | 2 tsp. |
| Paprika | 2 $^3/_4$" sockets | 2 tsp. |
| Pepper | $^1/_4$" socket | $^1/_4$ tsp. |

Chop the chickens into the usual parts. Toss the flour, salt, paprika and pepper into a Hefty garbage bag. Hurl in 4-5 chunks of chicken and dance around your garage shaking the bag above your head until chicken parts are fully coated. Place the coated parts in a hot buttered paint try and brown both sides. Transfer the browned parts from the paint tray to an oil drain pan or roaster. Torch or bake at 350° for 60-70 minutes.

41

# Hacksaw Chicken and Rice Casserole

You opened your big mouth and announced that you would fix dinner tonight all by yourself. Now, you have to deliver. Relax. You're a stud with a hacksaw.

**Tools required**: Hacksaw, oil pan, coffee can

| Ingredients | "Stud" measurement | Kitchen Equivalent |
| --- | --- | --- |
| Boneless & skinless chicken breasts | 4 | 4 |
| Poultry marinade mix | 1 pkg. | 1 pkg. |
| Brown rice | 1 full beer can | 2 cups |
| Cream of mushroom soup | 2 cans | 2 cans |

Cook the rice in an oil pan with about a beer can of water until water is absorbed (about 20 minutes). Meanwhile, prepare the marinade according to the instructions on its package. Hacksaw each chicken breast into halves and marinate. When marinated, place breasts on top of rice. In a separate coffee can mix soup and milk together. Pour soup and milk mixture over the top of the chicken and rice. Torch or bake for 45 minutes at 350°.

44

# Better Looking Finger Licking Chicken

This is chicken with great curb appeal. I like this one because it really makes us look like we know what we're doing.

**Tools required**:  Hatchet, paint tray, coffee can, paint brush

| Ingredients | "Stud" measurement | Kitchen Equivalent |
|---|---|---|
| Chicken | 1 whole | 1 whole |
| Honey | 1 shot glass | $1/4$ cup |
| Tarragon | $3/4$" socket | 1 tsp. |
| Butter | 1 thumb width of butter stick | 2 tbsps. |
| Grey Poupon mustard | 1 shot glass | $1/4$ cup |

Using your hatchet, whack the chicken into 8-9 pieces. Lay them in your paint tray. Mix the honey, tarragon, butter and mustard in a coffee can and paint your chicken parts with the mixture. Torch or bake at 350° for one hour.

# Bench Grinder Hawaii Chicken

Okay, hot shot, this one is ambitious. But, if you're getting the hang of garage cooking you may be ready for the challenge. Besides, if you get in the middle of this and screw it up, Domino's Pizza is only 30 minutes away.

**Tools required**:  Paint tray, coffee can, bench grinder, body file

| Ingredients | "Stud" measurement | Kitchen Equivalent |
|---|---|---|
| Boneless chicken breasts | 6 | 6 |
| Melted butter | 2 thumb widths of butter stick | 4 tbsps. |
| Salt | 1/4" socket | 1/4 tsp. |
| Pepper | 1/4" socket | 1/4 tsp. |

**Hawaii Sauce:**

| | | |
|---|---|---|
| Grated orange rind from 1 orange | 1 | 1 |
| Orange | 1 | 1 |
| Pineapple chunks | 2 small cans | 12 oz. |
| Raisins | 3 shot glasses | 3/4 cup |
| Cinnamon | 1/2" socket | 1/2 tsp. |
| Flour | 2 spark plug sockets | 2 tbsps. |
| Water | 1/2 shot glass | 1/8 cup |
| Soy sauce | 2 3/4" sockets | 2 tsp. |

## Bench Grinder Hawaii Chicken ... *continued*

Slather the chicken breast with melted butter. Shake on salt and pepper. Place in a paint tray or baking sheet and torch for 20 minutes at 375°. While the chicken is cooking, make the sauce. Use your bench grinder to grind the peel off the orange. Hack the orange into small sections. Add peel grindings and orange to a coffee can. Also add the pineapple chunks, the raisins and the cinnamon. Heat this whole sauce mixture until it boils. Stir a lot to keep from ruining your coffee can. After the chicken has cooked 20 minutes, pour this hot sauce over the breasts and bake for another 25 minutes at 375°. When chicken is done, place breasts (chicken) on a serving plate and pour the remaining sauce back into the coffee can. Now, add the flour, soy sauce and water to the coffee can and let this mixture come to a boil. It will thicken up. Finally, pour this hot, sticky sauce over the chicken and dig in. Then, take a nap. You've earned it.

# BEEF

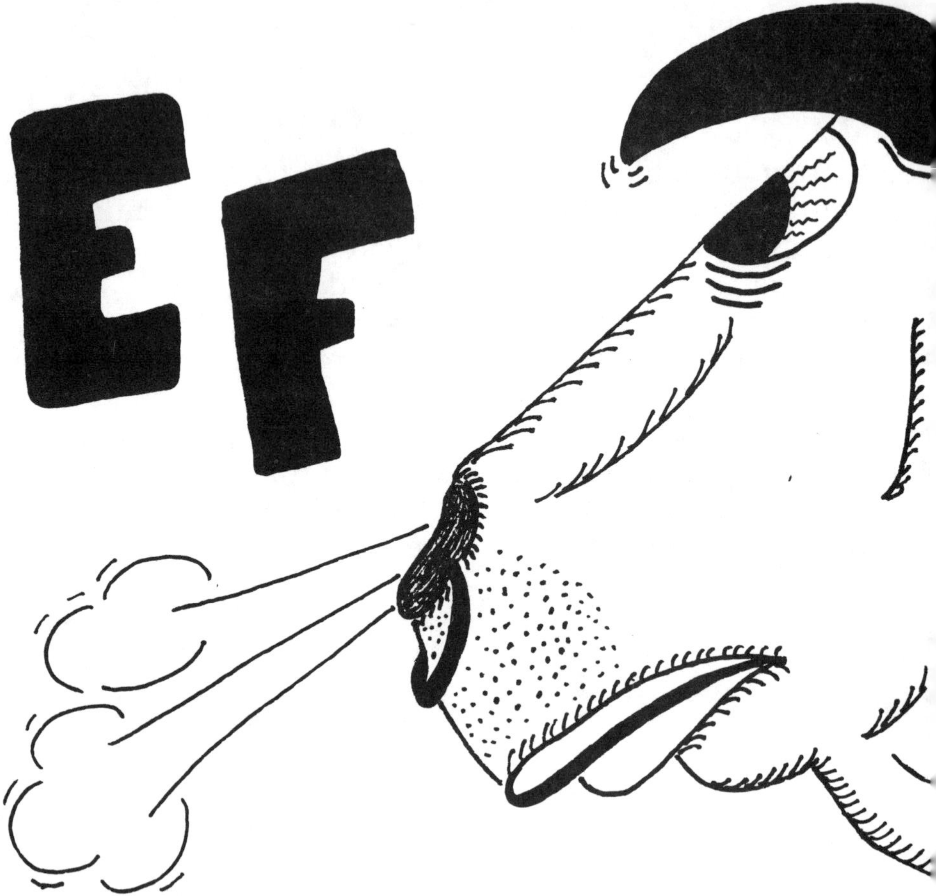

# Cheap Therapy Round Steak

Round steak takes a real beating in the preparation of this dish. Make this meal after you've had an argument with your wife or girlfriend. You'll get out your frustrations and you can kiss and make up over dinner. All for about 6 bucks an hour. No need to thank me.

**Tools required**:   Hammer, hatchet, paint tray

| Ingredients | "Stud" measurement | Kitchen Equivalent |
|---|---|---|
| Round steak | 2 lbs. | 2 lbs. |
| Wesson oil | 2 $3/4$" sockets | 2 tsps. |
| Cayenne pepper | $3/4$" socket | 1 tsp. |
| Salt | $3/4$" socket | 1 tsp. |
| Onion (chopped) | 1 | 1 |
| Green pepper (chopped) | 1 | 1 |

Lay the steak out on your workbench and hammer it until $1/4$" flat and tender. Use your hatchet to thinly slice the steak into strips. Hack up the onion and pepper, too. Heat the oil in your paint tray and toss in all ingredients. Fry for 2 minutes, flipping frequently. Serve as an open-face sandwich or main course. Send a copy of this book to your fighting friends.

# 2 x 4 Burgers Excellanté

I took a tip from Jeff Smith, the Frugal Gourmet, who taught me that no kitchen is complete without a hunk of kiln dried 2 x 4.

**Tools required**:   2 x 4, axe, body file, paint tray, paint brush

| Ingredients | "Stud" measurement | Kitchen Equivalent |
|---|---|---|
| Ground beef | 3 lbs. | 3 lbs. |
| Worcestershire sauce | 2 spark plug sockets | 2 tbsps. |
| BBQ sauce | 2 shot glasses | 1/2 cup |
| Onion (chopped) | 1 | 1 |
| Cheddar cheese (grated) | 3 shot glasses | 3/4 cup |
| Mushrooms (canned) | 1/2 can | 1/2 can |
| Salt | pinch *or* 1/4" socket | 1/4 tsp. |
| Pepper | pinch *or* 1/4" socket | 1/4 tsp. |

After you've chopped the onion with your axe and grated the cheese with your body file, massage them into the big lump of ground beef. Add the Worcestershire and mushrooms to the beef heap. Divide the burger mountain into 8 balls. Whack each ball with your 2 x 4. They will flatten perfectly. Paint on some BBQ sauce and cook over flame for 5 minutes on each side. 1 minute before you remove from the heat, warm your buns if they're cold. On second thought, don't cook burgers in the nude.

51

52

# Valvecover Meatloaf

The meal with an afterlife. Meatloaf sandwiches, cold beer and this week's *Sports Illustrated* are heaven to me!

**Tools required**:   2" putty knife, small block or V-6 valvecover, axe

| Ingredients | "Stud" measurement | Kitchen Equivalent |
|---|---|---|
| Ground beef | 4 lbs. | 4 lbs. |
| Onion (chopped) | 1 | 1 |
| Cheddar cheese (chopped) | 6 shot glasses | $1^1/_2$ cups |
| Milk | 2 shot glasses | $^1/_2$ cup |
| Salt | $^3/_4$" socket | 1 tsp. |
| Pepper | $^1/_2$" socket | $^1/_2$ tsp. |
| Eggs | 4 | 4 |
| Bacon bits | 1 shot glass | $^1/_4$ cup |

Hack up the onion and cheese with your axe. Mix it into the ground beef. Knead in the eggs, bacon bits, salt, pepper and milk. Pack the whole mess into a valvecover or loaf pan. Pour a little ketchup over the top. Torch or bake for one hour at 350°. Slice with chain saw and serve.

# Light Beer Roast Beef

It's about time! You knew I had to include a recipe using our favorite beverage. I wouldn't be a "stud" if I didn't.

**Tools required**:   Big oil pan, hatchet

| Ingredients | "Stud" measurement | Kitchen Equivalent |
|---|---|---|
| Chuck roast | 2 lbs. | 2 lbs. |
| Ketchup | $1/2$ beer can | 1 cup |
| Onion (chopped) | 2 shot glasses | $1/2$ cup |
| Parsley (chopped) | 4 spark plug sockets | 4 tbsp. |
| Light beer | 2 bottles | 2 bottles |

Put the roast into a deep oil pan or roaster. Add ketchup, onion and parsley. Pour beers around the bottom of the roast. Cover with foil and torch or bake for 1 hour at 375°. Cheers!

56

# Sledgehammer Swiss Steak

The first time I made this recipe I pulled a shoulder muscle. Of course I didn't want my friends to know I'd hurt myself cooking. I told them I was bullfighting.

**Tools required**:   3# sledgehammer, axe, coffee can, paint tray

| Ingredients | "Stud" measurement | Kitchen Equivalent |
| --- | --- | --- |
| Round or Chuck steak | 2 lbs. | 2 lbs. |
| Flour | 2 shot glasses | $^1/_2$ cup |
| Salt | $^3/_4$" socket | 1 tsp. |
| Pepper | $^3/_4$" socket | 1 tsp. |
| Onion (chopped) | 2 shot glasses | $^1/_2$ cup |
| Green pepper (chopped) | 1 shot glass | $^1/_4$ cup |
| Tomatoes (canned) | 1 big can | 1  8 oz. can |

Cut meat into 4-6 serving sizes. Mix flour, salt, pepper in a coffee can. Dump half this mixture over the meat and sledgehammer it into the meat. Turn over and sledge again with remaining flour mixture. Brown the meat in a hot paint tray for 15 minutes. Turn down heat and simmer for another 45 minutes. Now, add chopped onion, green pepper and canned tomatoes. Simmer another 30 minutes. That's it! Hose off your sledge and eat!

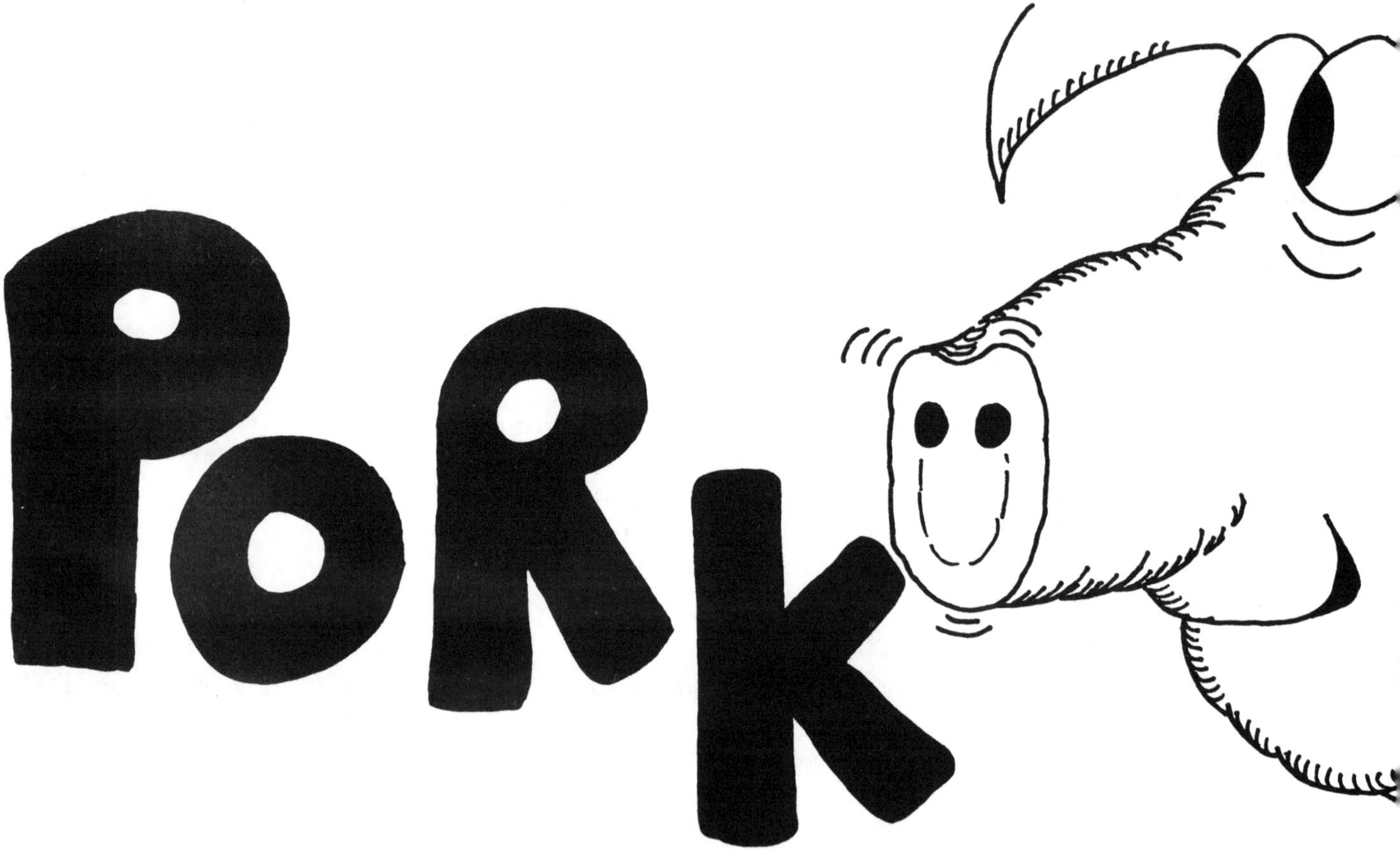
PORK

# Grand Slam Crosscut Ham

This is one of my Mom's favorite recipes. And, since my Dad has one of the all time great workshops and tool collections, I thought I'd dedicate this recipe to them. Chuck and Lois Shafer, two of the biggest hams I know.

**Tools required**:   Utility knife, oil pan, paint brush

| Ingredients | "Stud" measurement | Kitchen Equivalent |
|---|---|---|
| Ham | 5-7 lbs. | 5-7 lbs. |
| Brown sugar | $^1/_2$ beer can | 1 cup |
| Honey | 2 shot glasses | $^1/_2$ cup |
| Whole cloves | about 30 | 30 |
| Cinnamon | $^3/_4$" socket | 1 tsp. |

Put the whole ham on your workbench. Crosscut the top both ways with your utility knife about $^1/_4$" deep. Put the ham in your oil drain pan and torch or cook for two hours at 350°. After two hours stick a whole clove into each crosscut intersection. Mix the honey, brown sugar and cinnamon in a coffee can and paint the ham with this mixture. Cook the ham another 30 minutes, repainting with the glaze ever 3 minutes. One last tip — don't eat the cloves.

# Oh Baby, Baby, Baby Back Ribs

I always thought good ribs only came from some world famous restaurant. But they're easy! Now, my friends think *I'm* world famous. Okay, *I* started the rumor.

**Tools required**:   Paint tray, paint brush, coffee can

| Ingredients | "Stud" measurement | Kitchen Equivalent |
| --- | --- | --- |
| Pork ribs | 16 | 16 |
| BBQ sauce | 2$^1$/$_2$ shot glasses | $^2$/$_3$ cup |
| Pepper | $^1$/$_4$" socket | $^1$/$_4$ tsp. |
| Worcestershire sauce | $^1$/$_2$ shot glass | $^1$/$_8$ cup |
| Whole Potatoes (Russet) | 4 | 4 |

Place the ribs in your paint tray. Mix BBQ sauce, pepper and Worcestershire sauce in a coffee can and paint the ribs generously with this mixture. Wrap the spuds in foil and put them in the pan next to the ribs. Cover the pan and torch or cook for one hour at 350°. Take off the cover (probably foil) and repaint with the sauce. Cook another 20 minutes. Ribs & spuds are done and delicious. Don't have your cholesterol checked today.

# Skil-Saw Ham Steak

Now, we're taking the gloves off and putting the safety goggles on. If you don't own a power saw, sneak into a construction site. But remember, if my name comes up I'll deny everything.

**Tools required**:    Power or skil-saw, paint tray, 4" putty knife

| Ingredients | "Stud" measurement | Kitchen Equivalent |
|---|---|---|
| Ham | 5 lbs. | 5 lbs. |
| Wesson oil | 1 spark plug socket | 1 tbsp. |
| Water | $1^1/_2$ shot glasses | $^1/_3$ cup |
| Apple juice | 4  $^3/_4$" sockets | 4 tsps. |
| Soy sauce | $1^1/_2$ shot glasses | $^1/_3$ cup |
| Brown sugar | 3 spark plug sockets | 3 tbsps. |
| Ginger root | $^1/_2$" socket | $^1/_2$ tsp. |

Run the whole ham through the power saw so that you end up with 1" thick steaks. Heat the oil in the paint tray. Throw in your ham steaks. Toss in remaining ingredients and simmer for 10 minutes. Be sure to turn your steaks frequently or they will stick and burn. A drywall putty knife is a great flipper.

64

# Crushed Corn Chex Chops

You have to trust me on this one. I know it doesn't sound very appetizing but the Corn Chex people love it! It's good. Really. Really!

**<u>Tools required</u>:**    Utility knife, hammer, body file, coffee can, paint tray

| <u>Ingredients</u> | <u>"Stud" measurement</u> | <u>Kitchen Equivalent</u> |
|---|---|---|
| Pork chops | 6 | 6 |
| Crushed Corn Chex | 2 shot glasses | $^1/_2$ cup |
| Parmesan cheese (grated) | $1^1/_2$ shot glasses | $^2/_3$ cup |
| Seasoning salt | $^3/_4$" socket | 1 tsp. |
| Pepper | $^1/_4$" socket | $^1/_4$ tsp. |
| Egg | 1 | 1 |
| Milk | 2 spark plug sockets | 2 tbsp. |

Slice the fat off the chops with your utility knife. Mix the egg and milk together. Set aside. Use your hammer to crush the Corn Chex. Grate the cheese with your file. Combine cheese, Corn Chex, salt and pepper in a coffee can. Dip chops in egg batter and coat with the Corn Chex mix. Place in a paint tray and torch or cook uncovered for one hour at 350°.

66

# Hula Red Snapper

I grew up in the Seattle area. So, I've eaten more fish than Jaws. You will amaze people if you follow the two cardinal fish rules: Rule #1 — Don't overcook fish. Rule #2 — Don't overcook fish. Anchors aweigh.

**Tools required**:  Utility knife, paint tray, file

| Ingredients | "Stud" measurement | Kitchen Equivalent |
|---|---|---|
| Red snapper fillets | 2 | 2 |
| Soy sauce | $1/4$" socket | $1/4$ cup |
| Pineapple juice | 1 spark plug socket | 1 tbsp. |
| Ginger root | $3/4$" socket | 1 tsp. |
| Lemon (shaved) | 1 | 1 |

Combine soy sauce, pineapple juice and shaved ginger in a small coffee can. Put the fillets in your paint tray and pierce the fillets six times each with a utility knife. Pour the sauce over the fish and let soak (marinate) for 20 minutes. Torch or bake the fillets for about 25-30 minutes at 400°. Serve with lemon slices. If you overcooked the fish, they make good door stops.

# Salmon That Didn't Make It Upstream

You're in the big time now. You're about to make a tasty fish even tastier. Exotic spices. Aromatic ambience. Don't waste this on yourself. This is a woman pleaser. Call Kim Bassinger. Go on, call!

**Tools required**:   Paint tray

| Ingredients | "Stud" measurement | Kitchen Equivalent |
|---|---|---|
| Salmon steaks | 4 | 4 |
| Butter | 4 spark plug sockets | 4 tbsp. |
| Tarragon vinegar | 4 spark plug sockets | 4 tbsp. |
| Dijon mustard | 2 spark plug sockets | 2 tbsp. |
| Natural seed mustard | 2 spark plug sockets | 2 tbsp. |
| Dry mustard | 2 spark plug sockets | 2 tbsp. |
| Heavy cream | 6 shot glasses | 1 1/2 cups |
| Salt & Pepper | a little of each | to taste |

Melt butter in a paint tray. Add salmon and cook for 5 minutes on each side (medium heat). Remove salmon. Add vinegar. Cook 2 minutes. Add the mustards and cream until well blended. Don't let it boil. Bring the salmon back to the pan and heat two more minutes. Check your answering machine. I'm sure Kim is just stuck in traffic.

# Just For The Halibut

Cook this one right and it will melt in your mouth. Cook it wrong and I don't care. I cooked *mine* right.

**Tools required**:   Paint tray, coffee can, hatchet

| Ingredients | "Stud" measurement | Kitchen Equivalent |
|---|---|---|
| Halibut steaks | 4 | 4 |
| Lemon juice | 3 spark plug sockets | 3 tbsp. |
| Salt | $1/2$" socket | $1/2$ tsp. |
| Paprika | $1/2$" socket | $1/2$ tsp. |
| Onion (chopped) | 2 shot glasses | $1/2$ cup |
| Butter | 1 thumb width of butter stick | 2 tbsps. |
| Green pepper (sliced) | 1 | 1 |

In a paint tray, soak the fish in the lemon juice, salt and paprika for one hour. In a coffee can, melt butter and cook the chopped onion until tender. Put the halibut steaks in a greased paint tray. Top with the onion and slices of green pepper. Torch or bake at 450° for 10-12 minutes.

# Oil Pan Crab & Shrimp Casserole

This recipe looks complicated but it's not. You throw all the ingredients in a small block oil pan and let it cook while you watch Match Game. Think of this as your parting gift from me.

**Tools required**:   Axe, oil pan

| Ingredients | "Stud" measurement | Kitchen Equivalent |
|---|---|---|
| Dungeness Crab | 1 lb. | 1 lb. |
| Small Bay Shrimp | 1 lb. | 1 lb. |
| Green pepper (chopped) | 1 full beer can | 2 cups |
| Onion (chopped) | 1/2 beer can | 1 cup |
| Celery (chopped) | 2 full beer cans | 4 cups |
| Mayonnaise | 6 shot glasses | 1 1/2 cup |
| Worcestershire sauce | 6 3/4" sockets | 6 tsps. |
| Salt | 2 3/4" sockets | 2 tsps. |
| White pepper | 3/4" socket | 1 tsp. |
| Soft bread (cut into cubes) | 1 1/2 beer cans | 3 cups |
| Butter (melted) | 4 spark plug sockets | 4 tbsp. |

Mix all ingredients together except bread and butter. Spread into the oil pan. Now, toss in the bread and pour melted butter over it all. Torch or bake for 30 minutes at 350°. This is good served over minute rice.

# CHANGE-O-PACE

# Real Men Cook Quiche

My friend Bruce Fierstein wrote the book *Real Men Don't Eat Quiche*. But, he never said we couldn't cook it! In fact, real stud men not only cook quiche, we hold our wives' purses while they try on clothes.

**Tools required**: Hatchet, paint tray, coffee can, power drill

| Ingredients | "Stud" measurement | Kitchen Equivalent |
|---|---|---|
| Crab meat | $^1/_2$ beer can | 1 cup |
| Swiss cheese | $^1/_2$ beer can | 1 cup |
| Mayonnaise | 2 shot glasses | $^1/_2$ cup |
| Milk | 2 shot glasses | $^1/_2$ cup |
| Flour | 2 spark plug sockets | 2 tbsp. |
| Eggs (beaten) | 2 | 2 |
| Green onion (chopped) | 1 | 1 |
| Pie crust (pre-fab) | 1 | 1 |

In a coffee can, combine eggs, mayo, milk, flour and onions. Add crab meat and cheese. Pour it all into a pre-fab pie crust you can get at any supermarket. Place in your paint tray and torch or bake for 40 minutes at 350°.

# Machete Macaroni & Cheese

You'll never go back to the packaged stuff again. This recipe will stick to your ribs, your pan, your walls, and your dog.

**Tools required**:   Machete, oil pan

| Ingredients | "Stud" measurement | Kitchen Equivalent |
|---|---|---|
| Elbow macaroni | 1 tennis ball can | 3 cups |
| Onion | 1 | 1 |
| Butter | 1 thumb width of butter stick | 2 tbsps. |
| Cheddar cheese | 1 lb. | 1 lb. |
| Milk | 1/2 beer can | 1 cup |

Put macaroni in an oil pan of boiling water for 15 minutes. Machete the cheese and onion. Drain the water off the macaroni. Reduce heat and add the cheese, onion, butter and milk. Simmer another 8-10 minutes until everything looks gooey and chewy. Freeze what you don't eat and microwave later.

78

# Impress the In-Laws Breakfast

Cook for your in-laws and save yourself years of grief and aggravation. Next time they come to visit take time to make this easy masterpiece. From then on, your father-in-law will probably let you borrow his pick-up.

**Tools required**:   Utility knife or hatchet, body file, oil pan, paint tray

| Ingredients | "Stud" measurement | Kitchen Equivalent |
|---|:---:|:---:|
| **Part 1—** | | |
| White bread | 8 slices | 8 slices |
| Sharp cheddar cheese (grated) | 1 full beer can | 2 cups |
| Sausage (browned) | $^1/_2$ tennis ball can | $1^1/_2$ cups |
| Eggs | 4 | 4 |
| Milk | 1 full beer can | 2 cups |
| Dry mustard | 1  $^3/_4$" socket | 1 tsp. |
| **Part 2—** | | |
| Cream of mushroom soup | 1 can | 1 can |
| Milk | 2 shot glasses | $^1/_2$ cup |

Brown the sausage in a paint tray. Set aside. Cut off bread crusts and layer bread in the bottom of a greased oil pan. Add sausage. Top with cheese. Mix eggs, milk and mustard together. Pour this mixture over the cheese. Refrigerate overnight. In the morning, mix mushroom soup and milk together and pour over top. Torch or bake the whole thing for $1^1/_2$ hours at 300°. Start to think of uses for the pickup.

# Campfire Lamp Chops

Why anyone would take Lamp chops on a camping trip is beyond me. But if you did you could make these. Far be it from me to tell you how to camp.

**Tools required**:   Hatchet, paint tray, vise grips, paint brush

| Ingredients | "Stud" measurement | Kitchen Equivalent |
| --- | --- | --- |
| Lamb chops (1" thick) | 4 | 4 |
| Honey | 2 shot glasses | $1/2$ cup |
| Mustard | 2 shot glasses | $1/2$ cup |
| Onion salt | $1/4$" socket | $1/4$ tsp. |
| Pepper | $1/4$" socket | $1/4$ tsp. |

Use your hatchet to cut off the excess fat from the chops. Put the meat in your paint tray and hold with vise grips about 4" above medium coals. Cook 15 minutes on each side. While chops are grilling, heat the honey, mustard, salt & pepper in a small coffee can. Paint this sauce over the chops often. Meat should be juicy and slightly pink when done. Did you remember to pack the Dom Perignon?

# Cheaters Homemade Pizza

Making homemade pizza is admirable enough. But don't go crazy and try to make the dough yourself. We're stud men, not pastry chefs. Add or subtract from my list of ingredients.

**<u>Tools required</u>**:   Utility knife, machete or axe, paint tray, body file.

| <u>Ingredients</u> | <u>"Stud" measurement</u> | <u>Kitchen Equivalent</u> |
| --- | --- | --- |
| Chef Boyardee Pizza Crust (or other mix) | 1 | 1 |
| Pizza sauce (canned) | 1 can | 1 can |
| Mozzarella cheese (grated) | 2 lbs. | 2 lbs. |
| Olives (sliced) | 2 shot glasses | $^1/_2$ cup |
| Mushrooms (fresh) | 2 shot glasses | $^1/_2$ cup |
| Pepperoni (sliced) | 1 pkg. | 1 pkg. |
| Green pepper (chopped) | 2 shot glasses | $^1/_2$ cup |
| Tomatoes (sliced) | 1 | 1 |
| Onion (chopped) | 2 shot glasses | $^1/_2$ cup |

# Cheaters Homemade Pizza ... *continued*

Mix the pizza crust dough according to the instructions on the package. When it has fully risen, spread it out in your paint tray making sure the border forms a small wall around the perimeter. This wall will hold in the toppings. Pour the pizza sauce into the dough "reservoir". Toss in half the grated mozzarella. Arrange the pepperoni and two other toppings on top of the sauce. Cover with half of the remaining mozzarella. Throw on the rest of the toppings. Top with the balance of the cheese and torch or bake for 10-12 minutes at 450° until crust is golden brown. Cut to size with your utility knife. If you still feel the need to make your own dough seek medical attention immediately.

# Recipe Notes

# Recipe Notes

# Recipe Notes

# Recipe Notes

# Your Turn!

If you have a recipe you would like included in the next **Stud** cookbook,
please send it to:

**Jester Books**
**Cook-Like-A-Stud**
19818 Ventura Blvd.
Suite 333
Woodland Hills, California 91364